D1765322

U8

£2-99

The Eternal Dance

Kim Taylor Reece

"Every day I do not dance is a day off my life."

Friedrich Nietzsche

That quote was printed on a poster hanging on the wall of the studio of my Dance Master. The picture on the poster was of a circle of villagers of unspecified European origin, hand in hand, *en petit jete*.

For 13 years those words comforted and encouraged me as I studied ballet, modern, jazz, and ethnic dance in San Francisco and dreamed of a career in tights and tutus. My early teachers were of the old school... taskmasters who thought nothing of whacking a faltering student on the hamstrings. You could never do that today, of course, but at the time it seemed a common enough occurrence in any studio. I never resented the occasional birchstick on my backside because that was simply the price of perfection.

Every day I'd look at the poster while at the barre, bent in painful *plie*. I would bemoan the tedium of ballet regimen and envy the joyful abandon of the villagers, their complete freedom of structure. A few years and a thousand *plies* later I learned what all dance students eventually come to accept: true freedom is the result of relentless discipline.

That is why I'm so moved with the images in this book. Dancers are taken out of their element, away from the studio, and placed in unfamiliar and sometimes uncomfortable surroundings. They move without music, lights, or applause. They dance for themselves, a camera the only witness. The fact that the camera is in the hands of a fellow artist is no coincidence.

You would think that dance and photography are diametrically opposed media. One product is fluid, the other static. Yet the boundaries of each art are blurred here because Kim Taylor Reece understands dance as a creative process.

My Dance Master always liked to remind us: the power of movement comes from the solar plexus, the inspiration flows from the heart. These truths come to life on the pages of this book. The years of discipline and physical pain can be seen in the contraction of a muscle, the elation of flight on the face of the artist as she defies gravity with an exquisite 90-degree *grand jete*. Even in repose, the dancer radiates strength and charisma.

Whether in Red Square, Hyde Park, or on Lanikai Beach, the moments captured in the traditional Kim Taylor Reece black and white say more than any thesis on kinematics. They portray the essence of human motion through time and space.

This is artistry.

This is joy.

This is freedom.

Pamela Young

Pamela Young is a broadcast journalist in Honolulu. She has a bachelor's and a master's degree in Dance from San Francisco State University, and was a principal dancer with modern and classical performing arts companies in New York, San Francisco, and Los Angeles.

When I first came to Hawaii thirty years ago, I worked with ballet dancers in the studio. Then a thought occurred to me: "I'm in the Islands, I should be working with the dance of Hawaii."

The result has been decades of the most rewarding work imaginable. And over the years I compiled two collections of award-winning hula. Placing hula dancers on the beach allowed me to capture the elegance of the subject in a natural environment.

Now I've come full-circle, back to ballet and modern dance. It seemed instinctive to free the dancers from the confines of the stage, the barre, and the choreography. The result is extraordinary and the reason that art defines me.

My goal is to create visual images that amaze me. Images that can be visited time and time again. Images that inspire. Images that are indelible. Images that are passionate. For me that is the purpose and the passion of art.

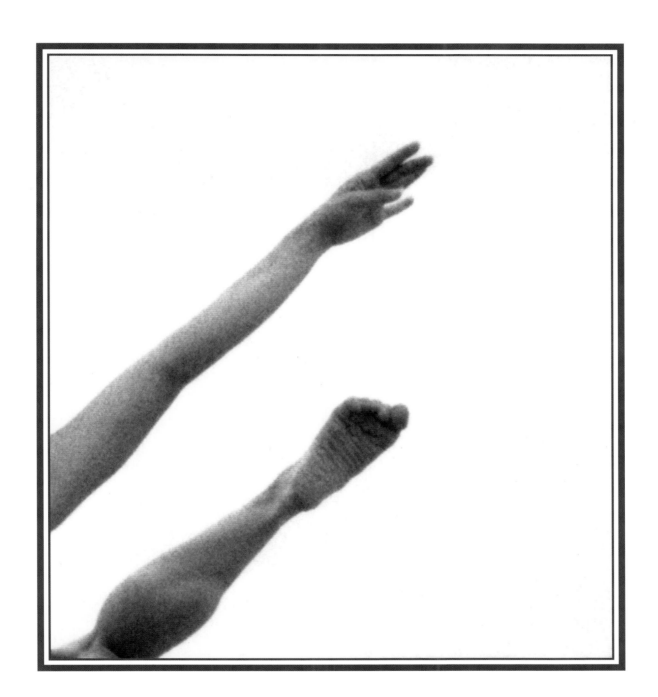

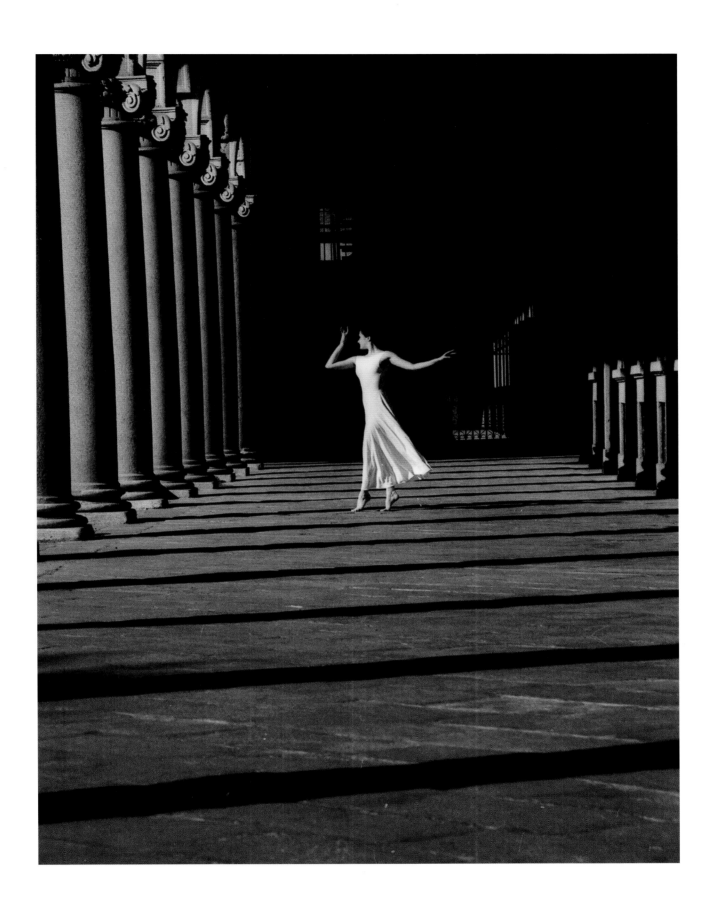

108

ACKNOWLEDGEMENTS

Mahalo Nui Loa

To the dancers who allow me to capture their grace and beauty and be
an audience to their artistry:
Rachel Berman
Sandra Brown
Rebecca Butler
Yukie Fujimoto
Heather Haar
Charlaine Katsuyoshi
Yael Levitin
Daniela Martin
Mareva Minerbi
Kamakoa Page
Marina Rzharmikova
Monica Violetti;

to Marc Myer whose incredible eye for beauty and structure offers the
coolest contributions to my work;

to Pamela Young for a great introduction, for understanding my art and
offering her time

to Steven Goldsberry for his incredible understanding and generosity of
language.

to my partner Kanoe who without her support and encouragement and
hard work my dreams would not be realized.

Copyright © 2006
Kim Taylor Reece Productions
Sacred Falls, Hawaii, USA.

All rights reserved under universal copyright convention.
No part of this book may be reproduced or transmitted in any form by any means, electronic
or mechanical, including photocopying, rercording or by any information storage or retrieval
system, without express written consent from the publisher or copyright holder.

Kim Taylor Reece Gallery
53-866 Kamehameha Highway, Scared Falls, Hawai'i 96717

www.kimtaylorreece.com

ISBN 1-59779-028-1

Printed in China by Everbest Printing Co., Ltd.